KINGDOM OF GOD IN YOU

Evangelist

Harrison Johnson Uche

Copyright © 2016. All rights reserved.

No part of this publication may be reproduced, stored in a retrieval system or transmitted in any way by any means, electronic, mechanical, photocopy, recording or otherwise, without the prior permission of the author except as provided by USA copyright law.

All characters appearing in this work are fictitious. Any resemblance to real persons, living or dead, is purely coincidental.

The opinions expressed by the author are not necessarily those of Revival Waves of Glory Books & Publishing.

Published by Revival Waves of Glory Books & Publishing
PO Box 596| Litchfield, Illinois62056USA
www.revivalwavesofgloryministries.com

Revival Waves of Glory Books & Publishing is committed to excellence in the publishing industry.

Book design Copyright © 2016 by Revival Waves of Glory Books & Publishing. All rights reserved.

Published in the United States of America

Paperback: 978-1534962453

Table of Contents

CHAPTER ONE 4

CHAPTER TWO 13

CHAPTER THREE 18

CHAPTER FOUR 22

CHAPTER FIVE 26

CHAPTER SIX 31

CHAPTER SEVEN 40

CHAPTER EIGHT 45

CHAPTER NINE 51

CHAPTER TEN 59

CHAPTER ELEVEN 67

CHAPTER ONE

Genesis chapter 1 vs. 26 - 28

And God said, Let us make man in our image, after our likeness: and let them have dominion over the fish of the sea, and over the fowl of the air, and over the cattle, and over all the earth, and over every creeping thing that creepeth upon the earth.

So God created man in his image. In the image of God created him male and female created him them. And God blessed them and God said into them. Be fruitful and multiply and replenish the earth and subdue it and have dominion over the fish of the sea and over the food of the air and over everything that moved upon the earth.

In the above scripture God created man in his image and commanded him to have dominion, subdue the earth and multiply.

The first purpose God is for man to have dominion over the earth. Understand that having dominion means to reign as a king. And it is important to note that you cannot reign without having Kingdom. Thus for a man (you) to reign, he must have a Kingdom.

Meaning that the first purpose of God concerning man is to make him a king here on earth so that man will rule as God is ruling both in heaven. "Matthew 6 v 10 Thy kingdom come. Thy will be done in earth, as it is in heaven.

And that is what we are going to discuss.

1. The original purpose of God concerning man which is make him a King and how man will receive back his kingdom through the gospel of his dear son. Jesus Christ.

2. The second commandment is to subdue the earth. The second purpose of God is for man to subdue any situation that is against the will of God in his life.

3. And third commandment is for man to multiply: meaning to increase in his blessings and become a blessing at a very moment of his life.

Note! That God positioned man in the east of Garden; this should draw your mind or attention to question, if there is another vision in the North, West and South of the Garden. So you should be mindful of the west, south and north of the Garden, though the Bible did not mention of another vision there.

Genesis 3 v 1-24: The snake was the most intelligent of all the wild animals that the Lord God had made. He said to the woman, "Did God really say that you shouldn't eat from any tree in the garden?"

The woman said to the snake, "We may eat the fruit of the garden's trees but not the fruit of the tree in the middle of the garden. God said, 'don't eat from it, and don't touch it, or you will die.'"

The snake said to the woman, "You won't die! God knows that on the day you eat from it, you will see clearly and you will be like God, knowing good and evil." The woman saw that the tree was beautiful with delicious food and that the tree would provide wisdom, so she took some of its fruit and ate it, and also gave some to her husband, who was with her, and he ate it. Then they both saw clearly and knew that they were naked. So they sewed fig leaves together and made garments for themselves.

During that day's cool evening breeze, they heard the sound of the Lord God walking in the garden; and the man and his wife hid themselves from the Lord God in the middle of the garden's trees. The Lord God called to the man and said to him, "Where are you?"

The man replied, "I heard your sound in the garden; I was afraid because I was naked, and I hid myself."

He said, "Who told you that you were naked? Did you eat from the tree, which I commanded you not to eat?" The man said, "The woman you gave me, she gave me some fruit from the tree, and I ate. The Lord God said to the woman, "What have you done?!" And the woman said, "The snake tricked me, and I ate."

The Lord God said to the snake, «Because you did this, you are the one cursed out of all the farm animals, out of all the wild animals. On your belly you will crawl and dust you will eat very day of your life. I will put contempt between you and the woman, between your offspring and hers.

They will strike your head, but you will strike at their heels." To the woman he said,

"I will make your pregnancy very painful; in pain you will bear children.

You will desire your husband, but he will rule over you."

To the man he said, "Because you listened to your wife's voice and you ate from the tree that I commanded, 'Don't eat from it,' cursed is the fertile land because of you;in pain you will eat from it every day of your life. Weeds and thistles will grow for you, even as you eat the field's plants; by the sweat of your face you will eat bread—Until you return to the fertile land, since from it you were taken; you are soil,to the soil you will return."

The man named his wife Eve because she is the mother of everyone who lives. The Lord God made the man and his wife leather clothes and dressed them. The Lord God said, "The human being has now become like one of us, knowing good and evil." Now, so he doesn't stretch out his hand and take also from the tree of life and eat and live forever, the Lord God sent him out of the Garden of Eden to farm the fertile land from which he was taken. He drove out the human. To the east of the Garden of Eden, he stationed winged creatures wielding flaming swords to guard the way to the tree of life.

From the above two scripture, we understood that God created men with a purpose to make him King over all his creation but because of disobedience, man lost that opportunity to the devil and bring condemnation, death unto himself.

Roman 5v12: Just as through one human being sin came into the world, and death came through sin, so death has come to everyone, since everyone has sinned.

Making sin and death to rule over man that supposes to subdue and have them under his control. Sin and death reign from disobedience of Adam till the time of Moses.

Though commandment (law) was given by God to Moses, the commandment could not restore back man's lost glory and kingdom.

Hebrews 7 v 19: Because the Law made nothing perfect. On the other hand, a better hope is introduced, through which we draw near to God.

God have to look for a better platform to make sure that he restores man back to his original purpose, where man will be made free from sin and captive of the devil. Having giving the law in Moses and the law could not restore back the kingdom to man and place him as the king that God wanted him to be.

Hebrews9 V 1:12, so then the first covenant had regulations for the priests' service and the holy place on earth. They pitched the first tent called the holy place. It contained the lampstand, the table, and the loaves of bread presented to God.

There was a tent behind the second curtain called the holy of holies. 4It had the gold altar for incense and the chest containing the covenant, which was covered with gold on all sides. In the chest there was a gold jar containing manna, Aaron's rod that budded, and the stone tablets of the covenant.

Above the chest there were magnificent winged creatures casting their shadow over the seat of the chest, where sin is taken care of. Right now we can't talk about these things in detail. When these things have been prepared in this way, priests enter the first tent all the time as they perform their service.

But only the high priest enters the second tent once a year. He never does this without blood, which he offers for himself and for the sins the people committed in ignorance. With this, the Holy Spirit is showing that the way into the holy place hadn't been revealed yet while the first tent was standing. This is a symbol for the present time. It shows that the gifts and sacrifices that are being offered can't perfect the conscience of the one who is serving. These are superficial regulations that are only about food, drink, and various ritual ways to wash with water. They are regulations that have been imposed until the time of the new order.

But Christ has appeared as the high priest of the good things that have happened. He passed through the greater and more perfect meeting tent, which isn't made by human hands (that is, it's not a part of this world). He entered the holy of holies once for all by his own blood, not by the blood of goats or calves, securing our deliverance for all time

For this reason God has to send his only Son to come and restore back the Kingdom to man.

Roman 5 V 18 So now the righteous requirements necessary for life are met for everyone through the righteous act of one person, just as judgment fell on everyone through the failure of one person.

Jesus came to fulfill the original plan of God which is to restore back the same kingdom that Adam lost by disobedience to devil at the Garden of Eden.

Jesus came so that, the same original program of God which he commanded man to have dominion over the fishes of the sea over the fools of air and over all the earth and over every creeping thing, that creeping under the earth, must be established and man will have his lost glory back.

God has designed it in a way that man will enjoy heaven here on earth, God created all the animal fishes of all kinds, fouls of the air and the whole earth for man to enjoy them here as a King and be glorify above everything situation on earth..

As God is king in heaven, so he created man to rule here on earth and have all things under his control as a king, Because in heaven God controls all, that is why he made man in his likeness and gave him the power to control all.

God doesn't want anything to rule over man, be it poverty, sickness, lack, limitation, barrenness, etc., that is why the Word of God declared, that God has given Christ a name above all other names, both things in heaven, on earth, under the earth, so that at the mention of his name all things must blow.

God doesn't want anything to control man, he gave his son Jesus Christ to save man from the bondage of any kind of sickness, lack, limitation, barrenness, and over everything that man cannot control or that is beyond man's ability to control.

Roman 5 V 6: While we were still weak, at the right moment, Christ died for ungodly people.

In order to make man King and restore his kingdom back to him. God has to send his only son as savior, to save mankind and to restore back the kingdom to man. And to start this process, God has to first of all introduce a massager in the person of John the Baptist in the book of Malachi 3 V1: Look, I am sending my messenger who will clear the path before me; suddenly the Lord whom you are seeking will come to his temple. The messenger of the covenant in whom you take delight is coming, says the Lord of heavenly forces.

.And in the book of Matthew 3 V1-2: In those days John the Baptist appeared in the desert of Judea announcing, Change your hearts and lives! Here comes the kingdom of heaven!"

He was the one of whom Isaiah the prophet spoke when he said:I will send my messenger ahead of you

The message or preaching of John the Baptist is simple 'Repent for the kingdom of God has come' To repent means to change from your old way of thinking, believe and understanding.

John disagreed with old religious teaching or teachers, he did not preach religion rather he was calling religious people both men and women to change from their old way of thinking and accept the kingdom of God which he John was announcing.

And that might be why he could not last long with the religious and political leaders, Matthew 4 v17: From that time Jesus began to announce, "Change your hearts and lives! Here comes the kingdom of heaven!"

Jesus also began his public teaching with the same message like John 'Repent, change your mind-set for the Kingdom of God has come' Underline that Jesus did not preach about his death, because his death is not the message. The main message of Christ is simple "the kingdom of God has come on earth." And he commanded his followers to preach the same message too.

Matthew10 v7: As you go, make this announcement: 'The kingdom of heaven has come near. Jesus warn that no matter your level or position, be you a pastor, prophet ,elder ,mother ,father ,youth leader you must preach this message of the kingdom that has come, stop preaching your own message 'The kingdom of God has arrive is the message you must preach to people listing to you.

Jesus said this because he know that there are other religious message that are capable of keeping people bound and far away from the track (God's original Plan) so he commands his disciples to change the mindset of the everybody from those messages that will not allow people from accepting and receiving the kingdom of God that has just arrive.

CHAPTER TWO

WHAT IS THE KINGDOM AND WHERE IS THE KINGDOM?

Many Christians would simply answers in heaven. But such answer may not completely be wrong, because God does reign heaven and on earth at the same time. (In the heart of his children)

So many Christians understood Jesus announcement of the Kingdom as an open invitation to get save and go to heaven without knowing why they are saved.

Part of their confusion or surprise comes from the fact that the gospel of Matthew records Jesus as speaking about the Kingdom of heaven rather than the Kingdom of God. Also in Mark 1:15 reads, saying, "Now is the time! Here comes God's kingdom! Change your hearts and lives, and trust this good news!"

Mark called it the Kingdom of God Matthews 3:2 has it the Kingdom of heaven. And saying, «Change your hearts and lives! Here comes the kingdom of heaven.

These phrases make many Christian to misunderstood Jesus teaching, to think that his announcement of the Kingdom was talking of something about God's ruling up in spiritual space or in the afterlife.

To be frank the Kingdom of heaven is not Kingdom that exists in heaven only but it means the reign of God over both heaven and earth.

The Kingdom that Jesus proclaims is in sense heaven on earth, not heaven in heaven.

This Kingdom has earthly reality that will lead to total freedom from, sin, suffering of all Kinds.

In fact the Kingdom of God is within you. A careful examination of Bible revels that the phrase, Kingdom of God, is nothing short of Gods will to establish his presence in the heart of men and woman through Christ here on earth.

Jesus said that the Kingdom is within you. God is within you, meaning that the greater part of the Kingdom of God exist in your heart. We can see that during of Jesus public teaching as he was responding to a question from the Pharisees about when the kingdom of God will come.

He made a remark that the kingdom does not come with observation nor will people say see it here or see it there. Therefore the Kingdom of God is within you. (Luke 17 V 20 - 21)Pharisees asked Jesus when God's kingdom was coming. He replied, "God's kingdom isn't coming with signs that are easily noticed. Nor will people say, 'Look, here it is!' or 'There it is!' Don't you see? God's kingdom is already among you."

This explanation of Jesus made it more simple and clear for you to understand that the kingdom of God is already within you and in your heart.

Jesus made it open to the Pharisees that in spite of their meticulous efforts, their mistake understanding would not allow them to see the Kingdom of God, because they think that the Kingdom of God will come with observation one day. And that is what so many Christian still think today.

Unknown to the Pharisees that Jesus who was in their mist is the King of the Kingdom. Therefore Kingdom of God turns out to be both in heaven and on earth, both which can be considering a very place.

What is obvious here is that this universe and everything in it is part of the Kingdom, while the other part of the kingdom is the spiritual or heavenly portion.

God's plan is to create a spiritual family for his only begotten son. He began this family with the creation of angels in heavenly or spiritual realm of it.

And he wishes this family not only to grow but also to be self-perpetuating. He explains this to us through the mouth of his prophet Isaiah. Isaiah 9 V7: There will be vast authority and endless peace for David's throne and for his kingdom, establishing and sustaining it with justice and righteousness now and forever. The zeal of the Lord of heavenly forces will do this.

There will be no end to the increase of his Kingdom (government) or of peace "is telling you that the government or Kingdom of God will continue to grow in peace constantly and forever in the heart of the Children of God "to establish it with righteousness and justices forever more.

Since Angels do not reproduce, the universal man was designed and created by almighty to reproduce. The Universe house the world we live in and reproduce on, which is the reason God, adopts his spiritual family from earth. Because reproduction allows a growth to his government.

Ephesians 1:5: God destined us to be his adopted children through Jesus Christ because of his love. This was according to his goodwill and plan

The body of Jesus was predestined but those selected to enter his body are not predestined. So God allow it at the free will of individuals to make the decision and accept the free gift of the Kingdom or to reject it.

The gospel of this Kingdom was the heart or core root of Jesus Christ earthly message. But many of his listeners fail to understand the mysteries of this Kingdom and their inability to understand that the Kingdom of God is within them prompt Jesus to spoke so many parables to them.

In that same manner so many Christian today are still waiting to observe the Kingdom of God when it will come with observation without realizing that the Kingdom of God is in them already.

Let's examine some of the parables used by Jesus Christ to explain the Kingdom and what it means to us as Christians.

A. THE PARABLE OF MUSTARD SEED

Matthew 13 V 31 – 32: He told another parable to them: "The kingdom of heaven is like a mustard seed that someone took and planted in his field. It's the smallest of all seeds. But when it's grown, it's the largest of all vegetable plants. It becomes a tree so that the birds in the sky come and nest in its branches.

B. THE PARABLE OF FIELD

Matthew 13 V 44:"The kingdom of heaven is like a treasure that somebody hid in a field, which someone else found and covered up. Full of joy, the finder sold everything and bought that field...

C. THE PARABLE OF A MERCHANT

Matthew 13 V 45-46:"Again, the kingdom of heaven is like a merchant in search of fine pearls. 46When he found one very precious pearl, he went and sold all that he owned and bought it.

And Jesus was preaching this Kingdom thought his earthly Ministry that he has come to restore back the same Kingdom that Adam lost back to man, so that man can reign again here on earth.

Revelation 5 V 9 –10: They took up a new song, saying, "You are worthy to take the scroll and open its seals, because you were slain, and by your blood you purchased for God persons from every tribe, language, people, and nation. You made them a kingdom and priests to our God, and they will rule on earth."

Christ purchased men and women with his blood that they may rule and reign here on earth and they cannot rein without them a kingdom.

CHAPTER THREE

Mysteries behind the Teaching of the Kingdom

Many Christian today still does not understand the mysteries behind the teaching of this Kingdom of God and that is why you see many Christian dyeing in poverty lack, want, sickness of all kinds.

In fact, the inability of many Christian to understand the mysteries of the kingdom and the purpose of Christ earthly ministry, made them to believe that it is normal thing to be poor.

They believe that serving God in truth and in spirit has limited their chance of being rich on earth. Many of these type of believers believed that you cannot live like a King or be a wealthy man without compromising your Christian faith.

They see riches as devilish, to them hence the bible says that the love of money is the root of all evil, so having money is to sin against the Holy Spirit in their thinking.

This kind of Christians has come to the point, where they conclude, that there are type of money that a child of God cannot make on earth, because to their understanding, they believe that God cannot bless you beyond certain level in life as a Christian.

Thereby giving the devil the glory that supposes to be given to God, by their judgment, coming to God means to come and live in poverty and wait for eternal enjoyment in life after death (heaven) but from what we read in Revelation 5 V 10: It is the perfect will of our God to make us Kings and Priest, so that we will reign on earth.

This is the simple reason; why Jesus was slain. Jesus came preached this Kingdom of God to us and has paid the price to restore it back with his blood.

As a child of God you don't have any reason to continue living as slave to poverty, sickness, lack and any oppression of the devil.

Romans 3 V 24-26: But all are treated as righteous freely by his grace because of a ransom that was paid by Christ Jesus. Through his faithfulness, God displayed Jesus as the place of sacrifice where mercy is found by means of his blood. He did this to demonstrate his righteousness in passing over sins that happened before, during the time of God's patient tolerance. He also did this to demonstrate that he is righteous in the present time, and to treat the one who has faith in Jesus as righteous.

God want you to accept this message of the Kingdom, change your mentality and understanding and to believe that Jesus came to restore back the Kingdom of God to you, that is why he died for your sin and to receive the message of this kingdom.

Romans 5 V 6-9: While we were still weak, at the right moment, Christ died for ungodly people. It isn't often that someone will die for a righteous person, though maybe someone might dare to die for a good person. But God shows his love for us, because while we were still sinners Christ died for us. So, now that we have been made righteous by his blood, we can be even more certain that we will be saved from God's wrath through him.

And he was made poor so that you might be made rich though his poverty, his poverty takes the place of your poverty and gives you his riches, his wounds gives healing. This is a great mystery beyond human understanding.

So you have to accept this offer to become King by opening yourselves to the understanding to the mystery of the teaching of this Kingdom and you will receive your kingdom as your failure to accept it will leave you at the mercy of others to capture you in their kingdom. Remember that Jesus came to make people priest and kings that they may rule and reign here on earth and those kings must have subjects. So is either you accept to become a king or a subject to another king.

Matthew 13 V 10 – 13: Jesus' disciples came and said to him, "Why do you use parables when you speak to the crowds?" Jesus replied, "Because they haven't received the secrets of the kingdom of heaven, but you have. For those who have will receive more and they will have more than enough. But as for those who don't have, even the little they have will be taken away from them. This is why I speak to the crowds in parables: although they see, they don't really see; and although they hear, they don't really hear or understand.

Meaning to understand the mystery of the Kingdom of God is very important. As failure to understand it, will leave one wondering like those phrases during Jesus time that are waiting for the observation or sign of the Kingdom, without understanding that the Kingdom is in their heart or within them.

And by so doing, they deny themselves the opportunity to enjoy or believe the message of the Kingdom.

Matthew 13V 17: I assure you that many prophets and righteous people wanted to see what you see and hear what you hear, but they didn't.

This portion has made it more clearly to you that the mystery that God is about revealing to you through this Book is awesome and that many righteous men and woman in the past and in this present generation does not have the privilege to hear it or to receive such revelation. Of which if they do, they will gladly accept it. It is very painful and amazing that many so called believers have not come to the full understanding and mystery of the teaching of this Kingdom of God.

And by his mercy God has made it possible for you to come to this point and where he is revealing the mystery of his Kingdom though this book to you as a chosen.

Hebrews 12 V 25 - 28: See to it that you don't resist the one who is speaking. If the people didn't escape when they refused to listen to the one who warned them on earth, how will we escape if we reject the one who is warning from heaven? His voice shook the earth then, but now he has made a promise: Still once more I will shake not only the earth but heaven also. The words "still once more" reveal the removal of what is shaken—the things that are part of this creation—so that what isn't shaken will remain. Therefore, since we are receiving a kingdom that can't be shaken, let's continue to express our gratitude. With this gratitude, let's serve in a way that is pleasing to God with respect and awe

CHAPTER FOUR
HOW TO RECEIVE THE KINGDOM

The Kingdom of heaven is not the Kingdom that exists in heaven only, but the reign of God over both heaven and earth.

The Lord's Prayer confirms this understanding of kingdom of God to us. Jesus taught his disciples to pray "your Kingdom come, your will be done on earth as it is in heaven" Matthew 6:10. Bring in your kingdom so that your will is done on earth as it's done in heaven.

Note! you are to pray for the kingdom to come on earth too, so it is not only a place which you go after death.

For you to receive his kingdom on earth is God's original plan and his will is that man should rule on earth, as he (God) is king in heaven even so should man be made King on earth positioning God as the king of Kings. Jesus also equates the Kingdom with the will of God. 1 John 4 V 17:Herein is our love made perfect, that we may have boldness in the Day of Judgment: because as he is, so are we in this world.

Currently in heaven, God reigns and therefore, for his will to be perfectly done on earth. Means you should pray that God reveal your kingdom to you, so that you will fulfill his will by ruling as a King here on earth.

When Jesus said to Pontius Pilate during his trial "My King is not of this world" (John 18:36)

Jesus does not mean my Kingdom is not on earth but up in heaven. No In fact this is not what Jesus means. Two pieces of evidence make this clear. First the book of John 18: 36 reads "My reign is not from this world. Second the portion of John 18:36 explains but my Kingdom is from another place "Now my reign is not here." Jesus is speaking not of location of the Kingdom, but the source of his royal authority.

Unlike Pilate he does not get authority from earthly source (Cesar) but from God, meaning that Jesus was not seeking to use his divine authority to establish only another political State on earth. Nevertheless the Kingdom he announces is in a sense heaven on earth, not heaven in heaven.

Therefore the Kingdom of God is both in heaven and on earth. You will always enjoy the spiritual realm, with God, while he will give you the physical Kingdom to reign here on earth and that is your destiny as a child of God.

In conclusion of Jesus earthly ministry, Jesus commanded his disciples to seek first the Kingdom and the righteousness of Kingdom by so doing that all other things will be given to them.

Note! Jesus has earlier made a remark in the Book of Luke 17 V 20-21: Pharisees asked Jesus when God's kingdom was coming. He replied, "God's kingdom isn't coming with signs that are easily noticed. Nor will people say, 'Look, here it is!' or 'There it is!' Don't you see? God's kingdom is already among you."

The question to ask should be, if the Kingdom of God is in us, why then should Jesus command us to seek for the Kingdom?

The interested point here is that for other things to be given to you, you must find this Kingdom because as a King you cannot rule without a kingdom or outside your kingdom.

And if you find this Kingdom everything you need to reign there will be given to you. All you need on earth to be rich, healthy, great, physically balance is hidden in the Kingdom.

And it is the perfect will of God for you to find this Kingdom and be able to rule as a King.

Note, whenever a King leaves his Kingdom to another place, he becomes a subject to another King.

So is either you are King in your Kingdom or you become a subject in another man's Kingdom. And in another Kingdom, you cannot be honored as King; rather you will be reorganized as subject no matter your contribution to that kingdom. And the role of a subject in any Kingdom is mostly a life of suffering, complaining, while the king enjoy and order his subjects around.

That is not the will of God concerning your life and that is why he decided to give you his son Jesus Christ who has brought and paid with his blood to make you free from being a subjects to the devil and his sons who has been ruling over man from Adam.

The moment you find this kingdom, you will be financially fit to face any financial difficult that is making you to question the love of God over your life.

Finding this kingdom will give you the peace of heart that you can't imagine. The kingdom of God is a mystery that until you discover it, you can never please God or have peace, because without doing his will you can't have peace of mind here on earth, and you must become a subject to another kingdom as such you don't have your will to live on.

You maybe, a child of God, a pastor, deacon, elders but without finding the kingdom of God you will keep struggling, to please God and to live a righteous life, you will keep struggling in your marriage, finance, health, business, and career etc.

Jesus did not die so that only your soul will be saved; he died that you might be made free from all the whole operation of the devil. Poverty, sickness, lack, want, marital problems, limitation, on timely death is the reason, why Jesus dies to set you free from all these problems.

And the Bible says in John 8 v36: that if Jesus set you free, that you are indeed free because he has paid for all this and has given you victory and restores the kingdom to you

The kingdom of God is the only solution to be happy and worship God; the way God wants you to worship him is through this kingdom. That is why Jesus said you should seek to find it first and stop complaining. Your suffering today is as a result that you have failed to discover your kingdom

Understand that it is the perfect will of God for you to have your kingdom and rule your world. You can never rule in another person's kingdom, no matter how loyal you are, you are still a subject. So you have to make up your mind to find your own kingdom today.

Matthew 11v12:And from the time John the Baptist began preaching until now, the Kingdom of Heaven has been forcefully advancing, and violent people are attacking it.

CHAPTER FIVE

How to Discover your Kingdom

The mysteries of the kingdom of God is a secret that only God can reveal to them that fear him and are willing to obey his command which is the kingdom rule. Matthew 13V11-12: Jesus replied, "Because they haven't received the secrets of the kingdom of heaven, but you have. For those who have will receive more and they will have more than enough. But as for those who don't have, even the little they have will be taken away from them

Whenever you repent of your sins and are baptized and start following the lead of Holy Spirit, you voluntary place yourself under the laws and authority of the kingdom of God.

Colossians 1: 13 – 20: He rescued us from the control of darkness and transferred us into the kingdom of the Son he loves. He set us free through the Son and forgave our sins. The Son is the image of the invisible God, the one who is first over all creation, because all things were created by him: both in the heavens and on the earth, the things that are visible and the things that are invisible. Whether they are thrones or powers, or rulers or authorities, all things were created through him and for him. He existed before all things, and all things are held together in him. He is the head of the body, the church, who is the beginning, the one who is firstborn from among the dead so that he might occupy the first place in everything Because all the fullness of God was pleased to live in him, and he reconciled all things to himself through him—whether things on earth or in the heavens. He brought peace through the blood of his cross.

At times, I wonder how people think they can rule their world without God. Many people think that they can amend some part of their life without God. So they believe God in some areas, while they depend on their ability in some area.

Is not all about being educated, having a nice Job, getting married to rightful partner that will determine how far you will go in life. In fact is all about God and only him.

Many people fail to understand that nothing on earth exist without God, be it money, business position, power, career, marriage, nothing on earth can last without God.

That means for you to discover the mysteries of the kingdom of God. You have to subject ourselves to the laws of God, knowing that you belong to a different community (the church of God) and the holy spirit will help you to obey God's law, As his spirit of power and of love and of sound mind (2 Timothy 1: 7) and has given you the ability to live by God's laws even though you are still human with human weakness.

Those that are led by the spirit of God are sons of God (Romans 8: 14) This spirit will make you to begin to fear him and live by his law and God will see and accept you as his son, then reveal the mysteries of his Kingdom to you and you can then rule like him here on earth. Psalm 115 V 16: The highest heaven belongs to the Lord, but he gave the earth to all people.

The mystery of the kingdom of God can only be revealed and made understandable to the people that are willing to obey and fear God. So for you to receive the mystery of your kingdom you must be willing to obey him

Matthews 13 v35: This was to fulfill what the prophet spoke: I'll speak in parables; I'll declare what has been hidden since the beginning of the world.

Revelation 5v10: You made them a kingdom and priests to our God, and they will rule on earth." Matthew 13V17: I assure you that many prophets and righteous people wanted to see what you see and hear what you hear, but they didn't.

The church is waiting to observe the second coming of our lord Jesus. Yet they have missed the message of the Kingdom of God.

They start preaching the accomplishment of what Jesus did at the cross and forgetting the physical reason why Jesus died was to restore the kingdom of God to his children and make them Kings and Priest unto God.

Matthew 11 V 25-27: At that time Jesus said, "I praise you, Father, Lord of heaven and earth, because you've hidden these things from the wise and intelligent and have shown them to babies. Indeed, Father, this brings you happiness. My Father has handed all things over to me. No one knows the Son except the Father. And nobody knows the Father except the Son and anyone to whom the Son wants to reveal him.

The gospel or good news of the Kingdom is the message that Jesus urges you to believe today. Since he is the only being through whom you may receive salvation. Act 4v 12 Salvation can be found in no one else. Throughout the whole world, no other name has been given among humans through whom we must be saved."

You must heed his instruction to change your thinking and believe the gospel of this Kingdom Mark1:15 saying, "Now is the time! Here comes God's kingdom! Change your hearts and lives, and trust this good news!"

The gospel of this kingdom is indeed glorious news that will only determine your peace of mind, freedom for all the suffering and challenges of life here on earth and you will be free to worship God here on earth without being subject to anything as you will be in control of every situations.

You will keep struggling in your finances, marriage, career, Business and every areas of life until you discover you're Kingdom and begin to rule as designed by God.

God will reveal his Kingdom to you, the moment you begin to obey his commandments and follow his ways. Remember your own Kingdom on earth is different from another person's Kingdom that is why Jesus said that this Kingdom will not come with observation rather the Kingdom is already in you.

Luke 17:21: Nor will people say, 'Look, here it is!' or 'There it is!' Don't you see? God's kingdom is already among you."

As Jesus use different parables to explain these Kingdoms of God and how it is already in existence, also in the book of Genesis we understand that God kept Adam at east of the garden.

This will give you clear picture to understand that the garden has south, west and the north, though the bible did not mention that.

God is willing to reveal your Kingdom to you and establish you as a king if you are willing to obey and fear him.

Romans 16 V 25–26: May the glory be to God who can strengthen you with my good news and the message that I preach about Jesus Christ. He can strengthen you with the announcement of the secret that was kept quiet for a long time. Now that secret is revealed through what the prophets wrote. It is made known to the Gentiles in order to lead to their faithful obedience based on the command of the eternal God.

CHAPTER SIX

Call to receive the Kingdom

Call to receive the Kingdom is a call to righteous life and is a mandate to fear God and live in a sinless life in Christ. Is a call to amend or surrender your old way and be totally obedient to the word of God, then you will receive the kingdom

Romans 6 V 12-14: So then, don't let sin rule your body, so that you do what it wants. Don't offer parts of your body to sin, to be used as weapons to do wrong. Instead, present yourselves to God as people who have been brought back to life from the dead, and offer all the parts of your body to God to be used as weapons to do right. Sin will have no power over you, because you aren't under Law but under grace.

Only on this condition can you receive the kingdom from God, if you fear him first and recognize that he is God, that he sent his son to die for you, to save you from sin and to restore back your Kingdom to you.

The first step is to fear God, to fear him unconditionally because the fear of the Lord is the beginning of wisdom. If you agree to make him you're first thing in life, recognize that he is alive in you; he will reveal your Kingdom to you and bring you from last to first as well, because he is at the last to bring you to first.

Your Kingdom is in you; all you need is this wisdom that comes from obedient to God's word and he will give you understanding to know your kingdom.

1 Corinthians 2v6-16: What we say is wisdom to people who are mature. It isn't a wisdom that comes from the present day or from today's leaders who are being reduced to nothing. We talk about God's wisdom, which has been hidden as a secret.

God determined this wisdom in advance, before time began, for our glory. It is wisdom that none of the present-day rulers have understood, because if they did understand it, they would never have crucified the Lord of glory! But this is precisely what is written:

God has prepared things for those who love him that no eye has seen, or ear has heard, or that haven't crossed the mind of any human being. God has revealed these things to us through the Spirit.

The Spirit searches everything, including the depths of God. Who knows a person's depths except their own spirit that lives in them? In the same way, no one has known the depths of God except God's Spirit. We haven't received the world's spirit but God's Spirit so that we can know the things given to us by God.

These are the things we are talking about—not with words taught by human wisdom but with words taught by the Spirit—we are interpreting spiritual things to spiritual people.

But people who are unspiritual don't accept the things from God's Spirit. They are foolishness to them and can't be understood, because they can only be comprehended in a spiritual way. Spiritual people comprehend everything, but they themselves aren't understood by anyone.

Who has known the mind of the Lord, who will advise him? But we have the mind of Christ.

James 1 V 5–8: But anyone who needs wisdom should ask God, whose very nature is to give to everyone without a second thought, without keeping score. Wisdom will certainly be given to those who ask. Whoever asks shouldn't hesitate. They should ask in faith, without doubting. Whoever doubts is like the surf of the sea, tossed and turned by the wind. People like that should never imagine that they will receive anything from the Lord. They are double-minded, unstable in all their ways.

Proverbs 3v19: The Lord laid the foundations of the earth with wisdom, establishing the heavens with understanding.

Proverbs2v4-7Seek it like silver; search for it like hidden treasure.

Then you will understand the fear of the Lord, and discover the knowledge of God.

The Lord gives wisdom; from his mouth come knowledge and understanding.

He reserves ability for those with integrity. He is a shield for those who live a blameless life.

Now the question is; what is Wisdom? Wisdom is the perfect will of God at any point in time; God's fear leads to his wisdom (Perfect Will) that will reveal his Kingdom to you, but you must ask him this wisdom in faith, because without asking in faith you are not going to receive this kingdom from him

Hebrews 11 V 6: It's impossible to please God without faith because the one who draws near to God must believe that he exists and that he rewards people who try to find him.

So the first step is to fear him, which is the beginning of the wisdom or first process of receiving his wisdom, that will reveal his Kingdom to you and you shall then share this Kingdom which you received by wisdom with love to others and other things like money which is mostly the problems of many people today will be given to you.

Understand that the only thing you need to prosper here on earth is not money but wisdom, which is God's capital also.

Proverbs 16: 16: Acquiring wisdom is much better than gold, and acquiring understanding is better than silver.

Proverbs 8v14-31: I have advice and ability, as well as understanding and strength. By me kings rule, and princes issue righteous decrees.

By me rulers govern, and officials judge righteously. I love those who love me; those who seek me will find me.

Riches and honor are with me, as well as enduring wealth and righteousness. My fruit is better than gold, even fine gold; my crops are better than choice silver.

I walk on the way of righteousness, on the paths of justice, to provide for those who love me and to fill up their treasuries.

The Lord created me at the beginning of his way, before his deeds long in the past.

I was formed in ancient times, at the beginning, before the earth was.

When there were no watery depths, I was brought forth, when there were no springs flowing with water.

Before the mountains were settled, before the hills, I was brought forth; before God made the earth and the fields or the first of the dry land.

I was there when he established the heavens, when he marked out the horizon on the deep sea,

When he thickened the clouds above, when he secured the fountains of the deep,

When he set a limit for the sea, so the water couldn't go beyond his command, when he marked out the earth's foundations.

I was beside him as a master of crafts. I was having fun, smiling before him all the time, frolicking with his inhabited earth and delight

Jeremiah 10 v12: He hath made the earth by his power, he hath established the world by his wisdom, and hath stretched out the heavens by his discretioning in the human race.

Seeking for the wisdom of God means seeking for God himself

John 1v1-3: **In** the beginning was the Word, and the Word was with God, and the Word was God. The same was in the beginning with God. All things were made by him; and without him was not anything made that was made.

1 Corinthians 1:24: But to those called by God to salvation, both Jews and Gentiles, Christ is the power of God and the wisdom of God.

Many Christian today fail short of this knowledge that Christ is the Wisdom and Power of God that made everything, that what he expects from them is to seek for him first (His Wisdom)

But they are use all their time seeking for money, peace, and freedom which cannot be achieve outside Christ and the kingdom of God cannot be reveal to them because they lack his wisdom.

That is why Jesus said you should seek for his Kingdom first and all other things like money; houses cars, partner, healing salvation deliverance etc. shall be added to you because everything was made by his wisdom.

But it is unfortunate that so many Christian believes that seeking the Kingdom of God first will make them poor, so they sort to get other things first before seeking for the Kingdom of God.

And that is capital lie that Satan is using to trap many Christian and enslave them into poverty, broken marriages, lack, wants, sickness, diseases, depressions, afflictions.

That is the reason you see so many people (Christians) looking for miracles here and there. Many people are bias going from one church to another, one prayer ground to another, seeking for miracles from financial bandage, depression, healing from sickness, broken homes, lateness in marriage, and deliverance from demonic attack.

Because devil has blinded their eyes and has sold this lies to them, to seek for other things first before the kingdom, the same way he did to Eve at the Garden of Eden. Devil has prevented many people from understanding the teaching of our Lord Jesus concerning his kingdom, he made them to believe that seeking for the kingdom of God first is to help God rather than themselves, so devil told them lies that is better to seek to receive miracles from God and run away.

Understand that you don't need to look for miracle, when you seek for the kingdom first because your life will be filled with miracles.

Mark 16:17-18: These signs will be associated with those who believe: they will throw out demons in my name. They will speak in new languages. 18They will pick up snakes with their hands. If they drink anything poisonous, it will not hurt them. They will place their hands on the sick, and they will get well."

The above portion of the scripture is not limited to the men of God or pastors, prophets only but to all, that are leads by the spirit of God that work not after flesh.

Romans 8 V 14-16: All who are led by God's Spirit are God's sons and daughters. You didn't receive a spirit of slavery to lead you back again into fear, but you received a Spirit that shows you are adopted as his children. With this Spirit, we cry, "Abba, Father." The same Spirit agrees with our spirit, that we are God's children.

The wisdom of God teaches us, that children of God don't run after miracles, because signs and wonders will follow them. But to come to this level of knowledge, you must fear God and he will give you his wisdom that will make you King over everything on earth, like in your marriage, health, finances, career, business and provide solution to every problems of life.

The scripture made it clear that children of God perish because of lack of this wisdom. You cannot receive your kingdom without wisdom and you cannot receive wisdom without fearing God.

Lack of understanding of seeking for the Kingdom of God first, makes people go after money and miracles, refusing to understand that any miracle you receive without seeking for the kingdom first, will crash within some time.

el.harrison00@gmail.com

Jeremiah 17 v11:As the partridge sitteth on eggs, and hatcheth them not; so he that getteth riches, and not by right, shall leave them in the midst of his days and at his end shall be a fool.

If you get a miracle without discovering the Kingdom of God, you will be like the crowd during Jesus time, always looking for miracle and yet not satisfy.

Any marriage aside seeking the kingdom of God first cannot be smooth. There must be complaining here and there. And if you receive miracle of financial break through and get money without seeking the Kingdom of God, Such financial break through will never last, because wisdom will collect all the money from you back and you will be broke in midst of your days.

Proverbs 13V11:Wealth *obtained* by fraud dwindles, But he who gathers gradually by [honest] labor will increase [his riches].

But if you get wisdom first, wisdom will give you money and the money will last forever.

Wisdom is God to money; in fact wisdom is God himself. As you cannot claim to know everything on earth, that is how you cannot know everything about God. Wisdom is in everything, that is why God is everywhere but he must be on the good side of everything.

Proverbs 5v14 I was almost in all evil in the midst of the congregation and assembly.

CHAPTER SEVEN

Understand that before the foundation of the world wisdom was. Jesus said seek you shall find. And the bible made it clear in James 1 v 5: But anyone who needs wisdom should ask God, whose very nature is to give to everyone without a second thought, without keeping score. Wisdom will certainly be given to those who ask.

And is only when you understand God as wisdom, that he is in anything and everywhere, your fear for him will cause you to seek for him first in anything you do in life, and he will reveal his Kingdom to you, knowing that you will reign in that Kingdom with wisdom which is (himself) God.

In fact any area you fail in life or still struggling is the area you don't have or have not seek for wisdom. Because wisdom is God and you cannot leave him behind and survive on anything.

We have to take heed to Jesus instruction and seek the Kingdom first and we shall receive everything and they will remain.

Whenever you get married without wisdom (God) that marriage will not stand, if you give birth to Children train them without wisdom and those children will not be useful to you or to the society.

Understand this, that you need to fear God first, to receive his wisdom and stop running after miracles, because miracles will follow you when you get wisdom first, you will live a life of miracle when you first seek the Kingdom of God, mystery on how to make money well be reveal to you.

Do not be afraid of change. I wonder why so many people today are complaining of their conditions but they are afraid to leave that same situation and follow God by accepting the message of this kingdom.

They need God's help but they always believe that if they obey God's instruction, they will be poor. These types of people believe that all they need from God is miracle because, if they spend their time, to seek God, devil has already told them that they will lose many clients or what will they eat tomorrow and how can they manage to pay their bills. So they choose to listen to devil and because of people like this, Jesus said to his listeners in

Matthew 6 V 24 -34: No one can serve two masters. Either you will hate the one and love the other, or you will be loyal to the one and have contempt for the other. You cannot serve God and wealth.

Therefore, I say to you, don't worry about your life, what you'll eat or what you'll drink, or about your body, what you'll wear. Isn't life more than food and the body more than clothes? Look at the birds in the sky.

They don't sow seed or harvest grain or gather crops into barns. Yet your heavenly Father feeds them. Aren't you worth much more than they are? Who among you by worrying can add a single moment to your life? And why do you worry about clothes? Notice how the lilies in the field grow.

They don't wear themselves out with work, and they don't spin cloth. But I say to you that even Solomon in all of his splendor wasn't dressed like one of these. If God dresses grass in the field so beautifully, even though it's alive today and tomorrow it's thrown into the furnace, won't God do much more for you, you people of weak faith? Therefore, don't worry and say, 'What are we going to eat?' or 'What are we going to drink?' or 'What are we going to wear?' Gentiles long for all these things. Your heavenly Father knows that you need them.

Instead, desire first and foremost God's kingdom and God's righteousness, and all these things will be given to you as well. Therefore, stop worrying about tomorrow, because tomorrow will worry about itself. Each day has enough trouble of its own.

The basic instruction from Jesus here is for you to seek first the Kingdom of God and God will add all those things we are looking for to you. That means, without receiving the Kingdom, you will keep struggling to have what to eat, drink, what to put on and on how to achieve heart desire. Your fear of tomorrow will keep hurting you today no matter how good government policy may look or how attractive it sounds; it can't stop creating fear to you.

But to live above this fear, you must agree with this good news, teaching and disagree with the teaching of the devil that serving God will make you poor, rather believe that obeying God will give you all that we are looking or need here to reign as a King.

Nevertheless is impossible to receive the Kingdom from him without obedient to his word. Jesus advise us not to give that which is holy into dogs, neither should we cast our pearls before Swine, lest they trample them under their feet.

So God can only reveal the mystery of his Kingdom to people that are willing to seek him first, based on the fact that his fear is the beginning of wisdom, that will reveal his Kingdom to them and establish them a King of that Kingdom and they will rule as God with righteousness here on earth, making God The king of kings.

1 John 4 v 17:Herein is our love made perfect, that we may have boldness in the Day of Judgment: because as he is, so are we in this world.

The bible say as God is in heaven even so should his children be on earth. In heaven God reign with righteousness and establish his Kingdom with wisdom. So he wants you to rule like him on earth with righteousness and wisdom which is him.

On this condition, you will be like God on earth, being in control of everything. King Solomon is good example of this teaching. He obeys the commandment of his father to seek God first, he build the house of God before his own house.

He loved God with all his heart and willing to walk in the ways of his father David without compromise, when God saw that King Solomon is already to follow him with all his heart. He appear to him in dream and said to him to ask, whatever thing you want and God promised to give it to him.

Without doubt King Solomon ask for wisdom to rule his Kingdom which moved God to given him riches above all the kings of the earth.

Solomon asking for wisdom from God simply means, telling God to give me yourself. God is wisdom and with him, you will be above your fear, mates and control every situation of life. With wisdom (God) you will have a good marriage, riches, sound health and long life because wisdom will always direct you how to do things right and take right decisions, that you will not destroy you later or take steps that will not destroy your marriage, business, health, career.

CHAPTER EIGHT

Fear of the Lord

The fear of the Lord makes God to appear to you, as wisdom and whenever he reveals himself to you as wisdom, you will always live to depend on him in everything you do; you cannot struggle for anything in life. Because whenever you grown to a level where you understand God as wisdom, you will prosper and make exploit in everything you do.

As the bible declares that those that know their God shall prosper and make exploit, it depends on how you know him. People that know him as wisdom must prosper, be best among their equals, as king Solomon was above all others kings during his days.

You will not struggle to do right, when you know him as wisdom because wisdom will always teach you what to do, at any given time. Remember wisdom is the perfect will of God at any point in time. And when you do the right thing at the right time, you will stop complaining and you cannot cry of wrong decision or mistakes

The main reason, why many Christians are complaining today, is because; they are not getting the rightful result, because of wrong decisions. They fail to do the right thing and they get wrong result in return.

And that is what devil wants. He wants you to keep complaining and start thinking that God is not faithful to you or that God has abandoned you. God is faithful and cannot abandon is children, God said in Isaiah 49:15-16, "I will not forget you. I have your name carved in the palm of my hand." Meaning that any time God opens his hand, he sees your name. He remembers you; you are just struggling today because of wrong decisions and your inability to discover your kingdom.

Devil wants to make you hate God and yourself. His plan is to make you begin to look for solution, instead of to enjoy your freedom, which Jesus has made you free (pay for). Praying for miracle every day is not the will of God; our God is a loving father who has putting all things under his children's control and command them to enjoy the blessings.

He said that you should ask and you will have them.

Matthew 7 V 7-10: Ask, and you will receive. Search and you will find. Knock, and the door will be opened to you. For everyone who asks, receives. Whoever seeks, finds. And to everyone who knocks, the door is opened. Who among you will give your children a stone when they ask for bread? Or give them a snake when they ask for fish?

Our main problem here is that we have not ask for the wisdom of God, we have not seek for his Kingdom that is why we are not receiving answers to our prayer. We are bias asking God for miracle, which, supposed to follow us or added to us, if we seek for the Kingdom. James 4:3: You ask and don't have because you ask with evil intentions, to waste it on your own cravings.

So the best prayer should be oh lord, I need your wisdom to receive your Kingdom. Oh lord reveals your Kingdom to me. When you are ready to seek the Kingdom of God, God will reveal it to you with speed.

I Peter 3:12: The Lord's eyes are on the righteous and his ears are open to their prayers. But the Lord cannot tolerate those who do evil.

The Kingdom will only be entrusted to them that are willingly to seek for it and they will have it. Meaning God will not answer your prayer if is not in line with the Kingdom.

Matthew 6V 9-11: Pray like this: Our Father who is in heaven, uphold the holiness of your name. Bring in your kingdom so that your will is done on earth as it's done in heaven. Give us the bread we need for today.

The words of this prayer confirm the understanding of the Kingdom of God. Jesus taught his disciples to pray for your Kingdom come. Your will be done, on earth, as it is in heaven. Notice we are to pray for the Kingdom to come on earth, it is not a place we go after death only.

If you pray like this God will reveal the Kingdom to you and you will share the Kingdom, with righteousness to others and everything will be added to you.

You should as well pray for the will of God to be done on earth. The will of God is to reveal the Kingdom to his children by his wisdom and make them Kings of the Kingdom. And they will rule with his righteousness. Understand that the righteousness of this Kingdom is love.

When you receive the Kingdom and share it with love, you will have every other thing at your disposal.

The greatest commandment of the Kingdom of God is love. Jesus said that we should take example of our heavenly father that has no limit in his love towards mankind. Who made the sun to shine to all men.

Matthew 5 V 20: I say to you that unless your righteousness is greater than the righteousness of the legal experts and the Pharisees, you will never enter the kingdom of heaven. Matthew 5 v 45: so that you will be acting as children of your Father who is in heaven. He makes the sun rise on both the evil and the good and sends rain on both the righteous and the unrighteous.

Matthew 5 v 48 Therefore, just as your heavenly Father is complete in showing love to everyone, so also you must be complete. And you must love the Lord your God with all your heart, with all your being, with all your mind, and with all your strength. The second is this, You will love your neighbor as yourself. No other commandment is greater than these." Mark 12 V 30-31

Without being selective to others whenever you receive the Kingdom of God, you cannot receive other things (blessing) attach to the Kingdom, because It is the perfect will of God for his children to share the Kingdom, he gave to them to others in order to receive other things which he promised to add to them, if they seek the Kingdom and the righteousness of the Kingdom.

But so many Christians today are ignorant that their blessing is attached to love they share to others, they refuse to share the Kingdom of God in them and by so doing, the succeeded in keeping themselves in bandage of poverty and lack.

This makes them to only think of themselves and their family. What matter most to them is themselves and nothing more, Apostle Paul explain this in 1 Corinthians 13v5: says" That love does not seek for herself and that is not easily provoked and think not of evil to others.

1 Corinthians 13v1-5: If I speak in tongues of human beings and of angels but I don't have love, I'm a clanging gong or a clashing cymbal.

If I have the gift of prophecy and I know all the mysteries and everything else, and if I have such complete faith that I can move mountains but I don't have love, I'm nothing.

If I give away everything that I have and hand over my own body to feel good about what I've done but I don't have love, I receive no benefit whatsoever. Love is patient, love is kind, it isn't jealous, it doesn't brag, it isn't arrogant, it isn't rude, it doesn't seek its own advantage, it isn't irritable, it doesn't keep a record of complaints

The word charity means love with action, so when we receive the kingdom, we are expected to share it with action to others in other to receive other things.

Without this type of mindset that is in Jesus (God) that made him to love both his own and his enemies, you will keep being poor and you cannot receive the Kingdom or be a perfect King of the kingdom that God want you to be. He created you in his image and likeness, and you must be like him if you want to rule here on earth.

Also Jesus said we should pray for our daily bread. Genesis 3 V22-24: The Lord God said, "The human being has now become like one of us, knowing good and evil." Now, so he doesn't stretch out his hand and take also from the tree of life and eat and live forever, the Lord God sent him out of the Garden of Eden to farm the fertile land from which he was taken. He drove out the human. To the east of the Garden of Eden, he stationed winged creatures wielding flaming swords to guard the way to the tree of life.

Adam could not eat from the tree of life in the Garden of Eden. (Jesus was tree of life in the Garden of Eden) And he was subject to death but because of the love of God, God gave his son to restore man back to his original plan, where man will live forever. He gave man his only begotten son and made him the bread of life, whosoever ate him will have life eternal.

John 6 V 35: Jesus replied, "I am the bread of life. Whoever comes to me will never go hungry, and whoever believes in me will never be thirsty...

John 1v1-5: In the beginning was the Word and the Word was with God and the Word was God. The Word was with God in the beginning. Everything came into being through the Word, and without the Word nothing came into being. What came into being through the Word was life, and the life was the light for all people. The light shines in the darkness, and the darkness doesn't extinguish the light.

CHAPTER NINE

Our daily bread

Our daily bread is the word of God that his children should desire each new day of their lives. Making the word of God a standard for your life, thus believing that you cannot do anything aside the word of God

And that is the level that God want his children to operate. He said that they should pray for their daily bread which the word from him every moment of our life.

Jesus further said in the same Matthew 6 v 48-58: I am the bread of life. Your ancestors ate manna in the wilderness and they died. This is the bread that comes down from heaven so that whoever eats from it will never die. I am the living bread that came down from heaven. Whoever eats this bread will live forever, and the bread that I will give for the life of the world is my flesh."

Then the Jews debated among themselves, asking, "How can this man give us his flesh to eat?"

Jesus said to them, "I assure you, unless you eat the flesh of the Human One and drink his blood, you have no life in you. Whoever eats my flesh and drinks my blood has eternal life, and I will raise them up at the last day. My flesh is true food and my blood is true drink. Whoever eats my flesh and drinks my blood remains in me and I in them. As the living Father sent me, and I live because of the Father, so whoever eats me lives because of me. 58This is the bread that came down from heaven. It isn't like the bread your ancestors ate, and then they died. Whoever eats this bread will live forever."

God drove out Adam from the Garden of Eden, so that he could not eat of the tree of life and live forever, because he has the seed of disobedience in him.

Today God in his love sent his son to restore back the lost kingdom to man through his death at the cross and for man to live forever as he created him in the first place, God made his son (Jesus) the bread of life and as many that will eat him daily will live spiritually forever.

John 15 v 1-17 I am the true vine, and my Father is the husbandman.

Every branch in me that beareth not fruit he taketh away: and every branch that beareth fruit, he purgeth it, that it may bring forth more fruit.

Now ye are clean through the word which I have spoken unto you.

Abide in me, and I in you. As the branch cannot bear fruit of itself, except it abide in the vine; no more can ye, except ye abide in me. I am the vine, ye are the branches: He that abideth in me, and I in him, the same bringeth forth much fruit: for without me ye can do nothing.

If a man abide not in me, he is cast forth as a branch, and is withered; and men gather them, and cast them into the fire, and they are burned.

If ye abide in me, and my words abide in you, ye shall ask what ye will, and it shall be done unto you. Herein is my Father glorified, that ye bear much fruit; so shall ye be my disciples.

As the Father hath loved me, so have I loved you: continue ye in my love.

If ye keep my commandments, ye shall abide in my love; even as I have kept my Father's commandments, and abide in his love.

These things have I spoken unto you, that my joy might remain in you, and that your joy might be full. This is my commandment, that ye love one another, as I have loved you.

Greater love hath no man than this that a man lay down his life for his friends.

Ye are my friends, if ye do whatsoever I command you.

Henceforth I call you not servants; for the servant knoweth not what his lord doeth: but I have called you friends; for all things that I have heard of my Father I have made known unto you.Ye have not chosen me, but I have chosen you, and ordained you, that ye should go and bring forth fruit, and that your fruit should remain: that whatsoever ye shall ask of the Father in my name, he may give it you.

These things I command you, that ye love one another.

From the above scripture you further understand that Jesus Christ who is the word of God made flesh is the true vine while his children are the breaches. So you can never achieve anything here on earth or prosper in the kingdom if you disconnect yourself from him by not eating him daily as your food.

Jesus also warned in verse 6 of above scripture that apart from that you will not achieve anything or prosper outside him, that you will also be cast out by the father to wither making it possible for other kings to capture you and make life a hell fire for you. Meaning whenever you are not eating from the word of God, you cannot be consider worthy by God to entrust his kingdom into your hand to enable you become a king rather another king will capture you in their kingdom and you will suffer as if you are in hell, because in another man's kingdom you must be a subject and serve him because they can never be two king in one kingdom.

So it is the best interest of God to reveal all this secret to you today, Jesus is the word of God made flesh and that is why he said whatsoever thing that I hear from my father I will made known to you through my word.

That is why Jesus said you should ask for this daily bread whenever you pray for the kingdom to come to you, because the word is the kingdom food.

God is still saying something today even in your situation, he still saying something about you, still telling you how to receive your kingdom. And you cannot hear him without first listening from his word. When all your desire is mostly for the bread of life which is his word and take your time to listen to him through his word, he will reveal himself to you, in any situation.

The scripture said that nothing on earth is made without him, Including your situation, marriage, business, everything that concerns you. Matthew 19 v 26: But Jesus beheld them, and said unto them, with men this is impossible; but with God all things are possible.

And if all things were made by his word, means it will be difficult for you to receive anything without him. He that made everything has the solution to everything and that is why Jesus said, that what is difficult to men, is possible to God.

John 14 v6: Jesus saith unto him, I am the way, the truth, and the life: no man cometh unto the Father, but by me.

Romans 5 v 17: For if by one man's offence death reigned by one; much more they which receive abundance of grace and of the gift of righteousness shall reign in life by one, Jesus Christ.) Where there is no way, Jesus which is the word of God made flesh says I am the way and through him all that receive the gift of righteousness shall reign in life, meaning when you have the word of God (Christ) you every died thing in your life will receive life.

All you need is to desire the bread of life, because with it, you will control every challenging of life, what makes the bread of life to give everlasting life, is the spirit of God behind the word of God. God is a spirit and those that must worship must do so in spirit.

You should desire the word of God than your physical meat.

John 6 v 27:Don't work for the food that doesn't last but for the food that endures for eternal life, which the Human One will give you. God the Father has confirmed him as his agent to give life."

Whenever you eat the bread of life you as your daily bread, you will have the seal of God the father in you. So you must to desire for this bread every day of your life to be like the father on earth.

John 10 v 30:I and my Father are one.

Whenever you have the seal of the father on you, you will look like him, as his image on earth, does the same thing he does, reason the way he reason, react to issues like him. No wonder Jesus said I am and my father are one, whosoever that see me, has seen him. People will see God in you, when you have his seal on you and you will be unstoppable, no demon or situation can stop you, your neighbors and enemies will come to you seeking for solution to their problems because whenever they see you, they have seen God

As God is in control of everything, even so shall you be in control of everything on earth, because of the seal, that you will receive, when you keep eating this bread of life. Bread of life, is all that you should depend on to survival whenever you receive the kingdom. When you have it, you have God's presence in you. And that will make you to act like God on earth. Heal the sick, raise the death, create your world, the way you want it and remember, that the bible says nothing was made without it.

Hebrews 11 v 3:Through faith we understand that the worlds were framed by the word of God, so that things which are seen were not made of things which do appear.

You need to receive this daily bread, to stop struggling and to please God, by eating it you will understand what the will of God in any situation is or what God want from you at any given time.

In fact, you will say like David Psalm 23: The Lord is my shepherd. lack nothing. He lets me rest in grassy meadows; he leads me to restful waters; he keeps me alive. He guides me in proper paths for the sake of his good name. Even when I walk through the darkest valley, I fear no danger because you are with me. Your rod and your staff—they protect me You set a table for me right in front of my enemies. You bathe my head in oil; my cup is so full it spills over! Yes, goodness and faithful love will pursue me all the days of my life, and I will live in the Lord's houses long as I live.

God will be directing you and you will not lack. He will restore your soul and you will fear no evil of any kind even in the table of your enemy. It is an error as a Christian to believe that somebody will kill you or is after your life. Demons do not dwell in the same place with God. If you eat the word of God every day, God will live in you and demons will run away because light and darkness can never stay in the same place.

The same John Chapter 1 verse 5, says that the word of God become light that shines in darkness and the darkness comprehended it not. Whenever you study the word of God every day, you will receive deliverance from all demonic oppressions. Marine husband or wife, evil spirit of all kinds will leave your body by force without even praying against them.

The word of God will become a light, and shine into your heart, all over your body and there will be no place for the demon to hide because no darkness will comprehend the light that will come from the word of God.

By studying the word of God every day, you will be free from every sickness, no sickness will be found in your system. Every agreement with hell shall not stand and covenant with death shall be disannulled. Because by his word you are heal. Eat the bread of life, to be healed from your sickness, to survive from every satanic attack or oppression. In fact you don't need miracle to prosper; you need the word of God only.

The word of God has all you need to prosper and your Kingdom can only be established by the word of God. God has given good voices to so many people, to sing good songs unto his glory and make money but because they neither seek for the kingdom, nor ask for the daily bread, which is the word of God nor for the will of God as instructed by Jesus.

They fail to understand that music is a Kingdom. So they refuse to share the song like their heavenly father to both the just and to the unjust. They are dying in poverty today; they are still waiting for the Kingdom to come by observation like the Pharisees.

CHAPTER TEN

From the parables of Jesus Christ during his earthly ministry in Matthew 13 V 31-32: He told another parable to them:" The kingdom of heaven is like a mustard seed that someone took and planted in his field. It's the smallest of all seeds. But when it's grown, it's the largest of all vegetable plants. It becomes a tree so that the birds in the sky come and nest in its branches." Jesus said the Kingdom of God is like mustard seed, very small which a man took and sowed in his field. When It growns, it will becomes the greatest among the tree, so that the birds of air will come and lodge in the breaches there of.

They refuse to share their song that God has given to them, songs that supposed to grow and become a mighty financial Kingdom, where they will live and rule. Proverbs 18 V 16: A gift opens the way for access to important people.

The same water you store in your house is the same water that another person packaged as bottling or sachet water somewhere and share to the world and makes millions from it.

Proverbs 11 V 24 – 26: Those who give generously receive more, but those who are stingy with what is appropriate will grow needy. Generous persons will prosper; those who refresh others will themselves be refreshed. People curse those who hoard grain, but they bless those who sell it.

The only different between the owner of bottling Water Company and other persons (you) is love. You are only thinking about yourself alone, you are thinking of using your water alone with your family members, without considering others out there or how to reach out to others with water.

While the bottling water company owner is thinking on how to reach out to people with water outside their houses, he knew that millions of people will not be moving around with buckets full of water on their head to their working places, markets or schools etc., So he decided to make provision to provide water to millions that will be away from their houses, that are without water and by so doing he will be bless and becomes rich by serving others.

Luke 6 V 38: Give and it will be given to you. A good portion—packed down, firmly shaken, and overflowing—will fall into your lap. The portion you give will determine the portion you receive in return."

When he sold a Sachet or bottle of water to you, you will give him money in return without complaining. If you consider how much, a bucket of water cost and how much you buy a sachet or a bottle of water, you will believe with Jesus in Luke 6 V 38: that you shall be given in double fold of whatsoever you give.

The more people you reach out with your product (service) with love the more money you make. Jesus gave this remark in Matthew 20 V 27: Whoever wants to be first among you will be your slave

Many at times the problem is that people want to exercise dominion over others. Nobody is interested to hear the word servant, forgetting that, it takes your love to serve others to rule in your Kingdom.

Your Kingdom starts from your services to others. But because you are thinking only about yourself that is why; you see yourself saving your money in the bank. For getting that the bible said proverb 11 24-26 that with bold, lead to poverty but he that scathereth will be increase and bless as well.

The funny part of it, is this, the money you are saving in the bank can never be enough to make you rich, and instead of you to use it and do something that will be useful to others and be blessed; so that the money will increase, you refused because you want to keep the money for only you and your family members and that is why you are poor.

The moment you beginning to think of what you will do, to benefit others, God will reveal himself to you as wisdom and give you a Kingdom to share without being selective to others. A Christian believer, unbeliever, pagan and Muslim can buy from pure water owner, drink and thank God.

Matthew 5 v 45: That ye may be the children of your Father which is in heaven: for he maketh his sun to rise on the evil and on the good, and sendeth rain on the just and on the unjust.

For if ye love them which love you, what reward have ye? Do not even the publicans the same?

And if ye salute your brethren only, what do ye more than others? Do not even the publicans so?

Be ye therefore perfect, even as your Father which is in heaven is perfect.

Jesus said you should love like God your father, that make his sun to shine to both to godly and ungodly that they may see your good work and thank your father in heaven.

Most of the songs you enjoy today in your churches, houses or offices, you don't know the writer of such song but you are enjoying them today because the writer shared it with love and you receive it freely. Think of products like phones, clothes, Radio stations, televisions channels, websites you use today they are Kingdoms given to men by God, which they sow and it grows into mighty tree today and you now depend on them.

The bible said every perfect gift come from God. The entire good things you are using on this earth today are gift from the God. And God is still ready to give more, if you are ready to eat him like your daily bread.

Devil and his agents (the rules of dark world) only make the people to believe that every good thing come from the water or marine world, which is capital lie, you can only believe such lies, because you have not eat your daily bread. God still want to give more schools, hospitals, Media house, and political power as a kingdom to them that are ready to eat him as their daily bread.

Kingdom of God is in you, seek it, receive it, sow it, it will grow and people will depend on it, but if you refuse to share it when you receive it, it will be taken from you and give to others. So ask you will receive your kingdom today.

Matthew 25 V 14-29: The kingdom of heaven is like a man who was leaving on a trip. He called his servants and handed his possessions over to them. To one he gave five valuable coins, and to another he gave two, and to another he gave one. He gave to each servant according to that servant's ability. Then he left on his journey.

After the man left, the servant who had five valuable coins took them and went to work doing business with them. He gained five more. In the same way, the one who had two valuable coins gained two more. But the servant who had received the one valuable coin dug a hole in the ground and buried his master's money.

Now after a long time the master of those servants returned and settled accounts with them. The one who had received five valuable coins came forward with five additional coins. He said, 'Master, you gave me five valuable coins. Look, I've gained five more.'

His master replied, 'Excellent! You are a good and faithful servant! You've been faithful over a little. I'll put you in charge of much. Come, celebrate with me.'

The second servant also came forward and said, 'Master, you gave me two valuable coins. Look, I've gained two more.'

His master replied, 'Well done! You are a good and faithful servant. You've been faithful over a little. I'll put you in charge of much. Come, celebrate with me.'

Now the one who had received one valuable coin came and said, 'Master, I knew that you are a hard man. You harvest grain where you haven't sown. You gather crops where you haven't spread seed. So I was afraid. And I hid my valuable coin in the ground. Here, you have what's yours.'

His master replied, 'you evil and lazy servant! You knew that I harvest grain where I haven't sown and that I gather crops where I haven't spread seed? In that case, you should have turned my money over to the bankers so that when I returned, you could give me what belonged to me with interest.

Therefore, take from him the valuable coin and give it to the one who has ten coins. Those who have much will receive more, and they will have more than they need. But as for those who don't have much, even the little bit they have will be taken away from them.

The message here is how many people can you reach with your Kingdom determine, how great your Kingdom will grow. Think of face-book, other communication companies, Media companies they make more money because they reach more people.

The same food and you eat in your house, is the same food they are selling costly in many big hotels around you.

But because you refuse to seek God's Kingdom, you don't receive the revelation of what to do with your food even when you know how to cook very well and you are still running around looking for miracle, that will give you a job in the bank out of this foolishness, another person will capture you and you will be subject to his Kingdom and work like slave.

Many Christians are complaining because of the rate of unemployment's in their country, they are waiting for a government policies that will create jobs for people, when they supposed to employ people in their kingdom.

Kingdom of God is differs, your own kingdom might be different from another man's Kingdom. But most important thing to note is that God will make you King and rule with you on earth.

In fact you don't need money to start your financial kingdom; you only need (Wisdom) God. His fear is the beginning of wisdom, not academically or worldly wisdom. And God's wisdom is only what you need to prosper and be king on earth.

1 Corinthians 2v6-16: What we say is wisdom to people who are mature. It isn't a wisdom that comes from the present day or

from today's leaders who are being reduced to nothing. We talk about God's wisdom, which has been hidden as a secret.

God determined this wisdom in advance, before time began, for our glory. It is a wisdom that none of the present-day rulers have understood, because if they did understand it, they would never have crucified the Lord of glory! But this is precisely what is written:

God has prepared things for those who love him that no eye has seen, or ear has heard, or that haven't crossed the mind of any human being. God has revealed these things to us through the Spirit.

The Spirit searches everything, including the depths of God. Who knows a person's depths except their own spirit that lives in them? In the same way, no one has known the depths of God except God's Spirit. We haven't received the world's spirit but God's Spirit so that we can know the things given to us by God.

These are the things we are talking about—not with words taught by human wisdom but with words taught by the Spirit—we are interpreting spiritual things to spiritual people. But people who are unspiritual don't accept the things from God's Spirit. They are foolishness to them and can't be understood, because they can only be comprehended in a spiritual way. Spiritual people comprehend everything, but they themselves aren't understood by anyone. Who has known the mind of the Lord, who will advise him? But we have the mind of Christ

Take a look at all the big churches around you or big pastors you know today, they didn't start big or start with money but they started with God and remain with him. God gave them their Kingdom (church) and they sow it, today the same seed has grown and make them millionaires without crime and they create jobs to others. They are making use of the same bible you keep in your house but because they are willing to receive their daily bread from God, they receive a different revelation and they keep receiving different results than you. They see God in his word because they keep studying about God, God keep revealing himself to them.

Many have not received the mysteries of this kingdom because they refuse to study the word of God. Matthew 13 V 17 for verify I say into you many prophet and righteousness men have desired to see these things which you see and have not seen them and to hear those things which you hear and have not heard them.

2 Timothy 2 v 14- 15 of these things put them in remembrance, charging them before the Lord that they strive not about words to no profit, but to the subverting of the hearers.

Study to shew thyself approved unto God, a workman that needeth not to be ashamed, rightly dividing the word of truth.

Apostle Paul ask Timothy to study to show himself approved by God because without having the word of God in you, you cannot receive the Kingdom of God. With our worldly wisdom you may receive vision that cannot be able to accomplish, you may set a goal by worldly wisdom but without the word of God it will not stand.

CHAPTER ELEVEN

How to maintain Kingdom wealth.

Tithing: Tithe is simply the ten percent of your increase. Paying your tithe does not help or enrich God rather it secures your financial future, it does not matter the amount you tithe with, but your knowledge about tithe is what matters.

Don't be deceived the day you stop paying your tithe, Life will become very tight for you and you will enter into debt. (Doing everything but tithe) If you do not pay your tithe, you are on your own. No matter how much you earn as wages it will not be enough to solve your problems, because you are robbing God. God requires faithfulness in your tithe not how much it is.

Malachi 3V10: Bring the whole tenth-part to the storage house so there might be food in my house. Please test me in this, says the Lord of heavenly forces. See whether I do not open all the windows of the heavens for you and empty out a blessing until there is enough.

Deuteronomy28v 2: All these blessings will come upon you and find you if you obey the Lord your God's voice

Continuous financial success is impossible in the Kingdom of God without tithing. If you do not pay your tithe, you are a total sinner because you are robber and have robbed God, and God will not allow his blessing to rain on you and you will not enjoy his Kingdom wealth.

When you do not pay your tithe, God will drove you out from your kingdom into financial wilderness where life will be so tight and you will lose direction on what to do. The truth is that it is impossible to enjoy the presence of God without tithe.

Genesis 2 V 16-The Lord God commanded the human, "Eat your fill from all of the garden's trees; but don't eat from the tree of the knowledge of good and evil, because on the day you eat from it, you will die!"

Also Genesis 3v23-24: the Lord God sent him out of the Garden of Eden to farm the fertile land from which he was taken. He drove out the human. To the east of the Garden of Eden, he stationed winged creatures wielding flaming swords to guard the way to the tree of life.

Deuteronomy28v 2: All these blessings will come upon you and find you if you obey the Lord your God's voice

God drove Adam out from the Garden of Eden into the wildness because he did not honor God's portion. He ate the portion that is reserved for God. God instructed them to eat of every tree but should not touch that which belongs to God.

Leviticus 27 V 30: All tenth-part gifts from the land, whether of seed from the ground or fruit from the trees, belong to the Lord; they are holy unto the lord

Tithe is the Lords portion and is holy unto him, so you dear not eat it, you can enjoy the rest nine percent, but not your tithe as Christian, your tithe is untouchable else you will die financially.

Do not add your tithe to your business else, your business will collapse, if you add your tithe to your marriage, you will have a broken home.

The day you use your tithe and pay for your child school fee, your child will start to give you problems, if you use it and buy drugs, the sickness will go and come back. God has already caused you and everything that concerns you.

Malachi 3 V9 You are being cursed with a curse, and you, the entire nation, are robbing me.

God will cause every nation for your sake, because you robbed him. Nothing will move well for you. Malachi 3 V 14: You said, «Serving God is useless. What do we gain by keeping his obligation or by walking around as mourners before the Lord of heavenly forces?

Therefore do not follow people that say, Tithe does not matter again, Tithe matters most in the kingdom, so made up your mind and be a thither, if you want to retain your continuous financial success in the Kingdom of God. God will grant you an open heaven that no man can close. Tithe is none negotiable if you want to keep enjoying financial flow.

2: OFFERINGS

Offering is whatsoever you give to God willingly from your heart, after removing your Tithe

Tithe is specific while offering are motivated by your love for God. Offering is showing your appreciation to God.

TYPES OF OFFERING

A. Kingdom project offering: This is the offering you give for building or house of God and other specified project in the church.

1Chronicles 29:3-5: What's more, because of my delight in my God's temple, I have dedicated my own private treasure of gold and silver to my God's temple, in addition to all that I've provided for the holy temple: three thousand kikkars of gold from the gold of Ophir, seven thousand kikkars of refined silver for covering the walls of the rooms, gold for gold objects, and silver for silver objects, to be used for everything the skilled workers will make. Who else, then, will volunteer, dedicating themselves to the Lord today?

B. **Prophetic offering**: That is the offering you gave to the men of God, the Vessel which God, is using to bless your life.

Galatians 6V 6: Those who are taught the word should share all good things with their teacher.

Hebrews 7: 7: Without question, the less important person is blessed by the more important person.

1Samuel 9V 7: Saul said to his young boy, "But if we go, what should we bring to the man? The food in our bags is all gone. We don't have any gift to offer the man of God. Do we have anything?"

2 Chronicles 20 V20: Early the next morning they went into the Tekoa wilderness. When they were about to go out, Jehoshaphat stood and said, "Listen to me, Judah and every inhabitant of Jerusalem! Trust the Lord your God, and you will stand firm; trust his prophets and succeed!"

A. **Welfare offering:** This is the offering you give to the less privilege, people that are in need more than you.

Proverbs 19 V 17: He that hath pity upon the poor lendeth unto the Lord; and that which he hath given will he pay him again,

Proverbs 28 v27: Those who are gracious to the poor lend to the Lord,

Proverb 22v9: Happy are generous people, because they give some of their food to the poor.

Luke 6V 43-45: A good tree doesn't produce bad fruit, nor does a bad tree produce good fruit. Each tree is known by its own fruit. People don't gather figs from thorny plants, nor do they pick grapes from prickly bushes. A good person produces good from the good treasury of the inner self, while an evil person produces evil from the evil treasury of the inner self. The inner self overflows with words that are spoken.

D. Free will offering: It is call free will because it will be given freely from your heart this is the type of offering you give in the church on service.

It is the type offering you give unto the Lord to appreciate his good work in your life, according to how he has blessed you. Never have you tried to come to the house of God empty handed.

Deuteronomy 16 V 16-17: Three times a year every male among you must appear before the presence of the Lord your God in the location he will select: at the Festival of Unleavened Bread, the Festival of Weeks, and the Festival of Booths. They must not appear before the Lord's presence empty-handed. Each one should have his gift in hand, in precise measure with the blessing the Lord your God gives you.

Matthew 5V23: Therefore, if you bring your gift to the altar and there remember that your brother or sister has something against you,

E. **Sacrificial Offering:** This is a seed, you sow in the house of God, which will grow and bring forth precious fruit to you and you have to sow that which will cost you great price.

Psalm 126: 1-6: When the Lord changed Zion's circumstances for the better; it was like we had been dreaming. Our mouths were suddenly filled with laughter; our tongues were filled with joyful shouts. was even said, at that time, among the nations," The Lord has done great things for them!" Yes, the Lord has done great things for us, and we are overjoyed. Lord, change our circumstances for the better, like dry streams in the desert waste! Let those who plant with tears reap the harvest with joyful shouts. Let those who go out, crying and carrying their seed, come home with joyful shouts, carrying bales of grain!

3. Our Character: Another way to maintain Kingdom wealth is through our way of life.

A. **Avoid waste**: Proverbs 19v18: Those who assault their father and drive out their mother are disgraceful children, worthy of reproach.

A wasteful spender does not enjoy supernatural supply from God. Waste of God's given resources will stop the flow of God's blessing to you, because God hate wasters.

John 6 11-13: Then Jesus took the bread. When he had given thanks, he distributed it to those who were sitting there. He did the same with the fish, each getting as much as they wanted. When they had plenty to eat, he said to his disciples, "Gather up the leftover pieces, so that nothing will be wasted." So they gathered them and filled twelve baskets with the pieces of the five barley loaves that had been left over by those who had eaten...

B. **Be modest**: 2 Timothy 2 V 10-12: This is why I endure everything for the sake of those who are chosen by God so that they too may experience salvation in Christ Jesus with eternal glory. This saying is reliable: "If we have died together, we will also live together. If we endure, we will also rule together. If we deny him, he will also deny us.

God knows your sizes; there is no need to live above your level in pretense. Do not fake life; stop pretending to what you are not. Just be content with what you have.

Philippines 4: 4: Be glad in the Lord always! Again I say, be glad! 5Let your gentleness show in your treatment of all people. The Lord is near.

Philippines 4 V 11-12: I'm not saying this because I need anything, for I have learned how to be content in any circumstance. I know the experience of being in need and of having more than enough; I have learned the secret to being content in any and every circumstance, whether full or hungry or whether having plenty or being poor.

C. Be a diligent worker: Proverbs 10 V 4: Laziness brings poverty; hard work makes one rich.

Nobody is born poor or rich, your choice determine what you become in life, giving or tithing without working is like pouring water into a basket with holes. Because there will be no channel by which your blessing will reach to you if you are not working or ready to work.

Proverbs 18 V 16: A gift opens the way for access to important people.

Eccl 5V19: Also, whenever God gives people wealth and riches and enables them to enjoy it, to accept their place in the world and to find pleasure in their hard work—all this is God's gift.

Proverbs 22:29: Do you see people who work skillfully? They will work for kings but not work for lowly people.

Combination of your giving and working determines your ultimate placement in life.

Psalm 1: 1-3: The truly happy person doesn't follow wicked advice, doesn't stand on the road of sinners, and doesn't sit with the disrespectful. Instead of doing those things, these persons love the Lord's Instruction, and they recite God's Instruction day and night! They are like a tree replanted by streams of water, which bears fruit at just the right time and whose leaves don't fade. Whatever they do succeeds.

John 5:17: But Jesus answered them, Jesus replied, "My Father is still working, and I am working too." meaning that there is no place for idle man in the Kingdom.

Until you are ready to work before you will be qualify to receive the Kingdom, and with diligent work, you will become a financial giant. Our God does not sleep nor slumber, he work day and night.

Isaiah 51:2 Look to Abraham your ancestor, and to Sarah, who gave you birth. They were alone when I called them, but I blessed them and made them many.

God commanded us to look unto Abraham, because he was diligent worker, God blessed him without measure.

Abraham receive and retain kingdom wealth and his prosperity continues with Isaac, Jacob, Joseph, Daniel, Solomon and with humbly people in the world like T.B Joshua, J.C. bright, Bill Vincent and my humble myself too etc.

These men receive and mountain Kingdom wealth because they understands that the mysteries of the Kingdom is in the word of God.

And if you will understand all these mysteries today, you will receive the mysteries of the Kingdom and maintain wealth therein. You will be called a righteous man. You will keep legacy for your unborn children as a righteous man.

The portion of a Righteous man

Psalm 112 V1-10: Praise the Lord! Those who honor the Lord, who adore God's commandments, are truly happy! Their descendants will be strong throughout the land. The offspring of those who do right will be blessed; wealth and riches will be in their houses. Their righteousness stands forever.

They shine in the dark for others who do right. They are merciful, compassionate, and righteous. Those who lend generously are good people—as are those who conduct their affairs with justice.

Yes, these sorts of people will never be shaken; the righteous will be remembered forever! They won't be frightened at bad news. Their hearts are steady, trusting in the Lord. Their hearts are firm; they aren't afraid.

In the end, they will witness their enemies' defeat. They give freely to those in need. Their righteousness stands forever. Their strength increases gloriously. The wicked see all this and fume; they grind their teeth, but disappear to nothing. What the wicked want to see happen comes to nothing!

The portion of the wicked Job 27 V 13-23: This is the wicker's portion with God, the inheritance that the ruthless receive from the Almighty. If their children increase, they belong to the sword; their offspring won't have enough bread. Their survivors will be buried with the dead; their widows won't weep. If they store up silver like dust, amass clothing like clay, they may amass, but the righteous will wear it; the innocent will divide the silver. They built their houses like nests, like a hut made by a watchman. They lie down rich, but no longer; open their eyes, but it's missing. Terrors overtake them like waters; a tempest snatches them by night; an east wind lifts them, and they are gone, removes them from their places, throws itself on them without mercy; they flee desperately from its force. It claps its hands over them, hisses at them from their place.

The choice is yours,
The End.

www.ingramcontent.com/pod-product-compliance
Lightning Source LLC
Chambersburg PA
CBHW052115070526
44584CB00017B/2497